Praise for

43 WAYS TO MAKE A GOOD MARRIAGE GREAT

Quick and easy—that's what I liked. Short chapters and a piece of cake to implement. Small book, but it made a big impact on my marriage.

— NOAH B.
CEO, BTI Developers LLC

The perfect gift for anyone—I could give this book to my friend, my residents, my mother, my boss, or my husband—and I know they'd thank me.

— MELISSA ROSENBERG, MSS, NHA

It's the perfect gift. I know a lot of married couples and finding the "right" gift that's meaningful and gives the right message is tough. Fortunately I found this gem. I love to give this book to couples that I know so I keep a dozen on hand.

— J. GOLDMAN
AUTHOR, *Secret of the Watermelon*

More Praise for
43 Ways to Make a Good Marriage Great

What a treat to read this book! In his own special way, with wit and wisdom, Mort Fertel takes 43 simple tasks and turns them into loving gestures. His first book, Marriage Fitness, was powerful and this is another "keeper."

— Rabbi Steven Krawatsky

Finally! A practical, precise and "points couples in the right direction" book. Couples need a no-nonsense approach to get quick starts that create lasting results. And this is it!

— Mary Ann Van Buskirk, M.A., M.DIV., LPC, and LMFT
Fellow of the American Association of Pastoral Counselors and Diplomat of the College of Pastoral Supervision & Psychotherapy

43 Ways

TO MAKE A GOOD MARRIAGE

Great

43 Ways

TO MAKE A GOOD MARRIAGE

Great

Mort Fertel

MarriageMax, Inc.
Baltimore, MD
www.Marriagemax.com

Library of Congress Cataloging information
Fertel, Mort.
      43 ways to make a good marriage great / by Mort Fertel.
      p. cm.
      LCCN 2010900128
      ISBN-13: 978-0-9744480-2-2
      ISBN-10: 0-9744480-2-8

      1. Marriage. 2. Man-woman relationships.
    I. Title. II. Title: Forty-three ways to make a good marriage great.

HQ734.F42 2010   646.7'8
                  QBI10-600011

First printing 2010.

MarriageMax, Inc.
Baltimore, MD
www.Marriagemax.com

In memory of my mother-in-law, Julie Breakstone.

May the merit of this book and the marriages that go from good to great because of it elevate her soul in heaven.

Acknowledgements

I first want to thank my five beautiful children for inspiring me. I know that the greatest thing I can do for you is to love your mother. This book is a result of my effort to come through for you in that way.

Thank you, Dov and Atara Frankel, Jon Goldman, Jody Bennett, Ephraim Goldberg, Emily Price, Daniel Ettedgui, and David Goldis. I appreciate your input and friendship.

Thank you, Randee Dutton. You did it again. I really appreciate it. Mom is lucky to have you as a friend.

Thank you, Barry Reeder. Your counsel throughout this project was invaluable.

Thank you, Rebecca and Adina. You are angels in my life. It's a pleasure to work with you. I admire your character and competence. Take pride in knowing that any credit I receive is partly attributable to your support. I simply could not do what I do without your help. Thank you very much.

Ari, my love. What can I say? You complete me. You are the center of my universe. I am blessed to have you as my wife. You are a woman of valor, an incredible mother, and the perfect wife for me. Thank you for your love, support, and friendship. Thank you for being my soul mate.

Finally, all my gratitude to the Author—it is my honor and privilege to serve as Your pen.

Table of Contents

Table of Contents

Introduction

*L*ove is not a feeling—it's something we do. We make a decision to love, and then we act. It's a choice and a deed. Love is a verb.

This book doesn't require much of an introduction. The title says it all. You'll find, in the pages ahead, forty-three quick and easy ways to make your good marriage great. In other words, this is a "how-to" book on love.

1 ~ Roll Out the Red Carpet . . . Here YOU Come

*I*magine you're invited to the Academy Awards in Hollywood. Not only are you going to the Oscars, but also you're arriving in the same limousine as Angelina Jolie and Brad Pitt.

For a few moments when you exit the limo, the whole world will see you on television.

How long would it take you to get dressed that night?

How many stores would you shop in before choosing your clothes for the evening?

Think about how you would prepare for the big night. Would you diet the week before, get a new wristwatch, spend a little more for a chic haircut?

I'll admit it would be a thrill to have the attention of the whole world for a moment, but wouldn't you rather have one person's attention for a lifetime?

You don't have to get an invitation to the Oscars to be motivated to look your finest. How about when you're invited to a wedding?

When we dress up, we make a statement to the person we're with that says *I think you're special—this occasion is important.*

Tell your spouse he or she is special. Get decked-out and transform an ordinary evening into an important occasion.

Honey, why are you all decked out?

We're going out, right? I'm dressed up for you!

REALLY? Wow!

Get Decked-Out

2 ～ THE INVERSE RELATIONSHIP

*L*isten to your breath twice. Go ahead and practice. This is for real. It will only take a moment. Listen to your breath twice and then read on.

If I didn't ask you to listen to your breath, you wouldn't have appreciated that you were breathing.

In fact, we're more likely to appreciate a good haircut than the source of our life. Why is that?

Indeed, human nature is such that there is an INVERSE relationship between frequency and appreciation. Simply stated, the more often something occurs, the less likely you appreciate it.

Breathing is a perfect example. Is there anything more important in your life? There's also nothing more frequent. When was the last time you were thankful for your breath?

Gratitude is a huge challenge in marriage precisely because of frequency. You and your spouse do so much for each other so often that you stop noticing.

You become numb to all your spouse's special qualities, but it's important to notice those special qualities. It's important to re-sensitize yourself. It's important to say *thank you*.

It's devastating to a marriage when people take each other for granted and don't extend the simple niceties (such as *thank you*) that they offer freely to complete strangers.

If your train of thought has you thinking, *oh, my spouse knows how appreciative I am*, forget it!

Don't kid yourself. Your spouse doesn't know if you don't communicate it. It never hurts to say *thank you*.

I suggest you do three things:

1. Make a list of everything your spouse does for you, your marriage, and your household. Also, list your spouse's good qualities.

2. Write a letter (preferably by hand) to your spouse expressing thanks for everything on your list. Be specific. Instead of saying thanks for planning family vacations, show your appreciation for the trip to Disneyland that your spouse planned to coordinate with your slow season at work. People notice when you notice details.

3. Give your letter to your spouse.

While we're on the topic of appreciation, let me take this opportunity to thank you. One of the strongest human desires is to feel useful. Thank you for using this book.

2   *Write a "Gratitude Letter"*

3 ~ How to Say, "I Love You"

I'm sure you have told your spouse hundreds of times, *I love you.* Sometimes, though, it's not what you say but how you say it that's most meaningful.

Have you ever been on the beach when a plane flies overhead dragging a sign behind it? I once saw one that said, "Julie, will you marry me?" Shortly after the plane flew by, I saw a woman jumping up and down with joy, screaming, and hugging her friend. I guess that was Julie.

Julie's future husband proposed using the same words as most men. The way he said those words, however, was special and Julie will never forget it.

This exercise has both an easy and a hard part.

The easy part is to tell your spouse *I love you.* The hard part is to do it in a way that is unforgettable.

An alumnus of the Marriage Fitness Tele-Boot Camp* sent me an email to share all the unique ways she said *I love you* to her husband. She gave me

*www.MortFertel.com/tele-boot-camp.asp

permission to share her ideas with you. I hope they inspire you and get your creative juices flowing. **She wrote the following:**

- I spelled *I love you* with canned cheese and crackers and left it with his dinner.

- I wrote the words *I love you* on the shower wall with dry-erase markers.

- I painted *I love you* on our rock, which he keeps with him always.

- I spelled out with peas *I love you* on top of his mashed potatoes.

How to Say, "I Love You"

Here are some other ideas:

- Text your spouse with the message 1-4-3, which is code for I love you.

- Make a photo collage in the shape of 1-4-3 or I love you.

- Hang a big I love you sign from your staircase.

- Make a home video of yourself singing I love you and play it for your spouse.

- Convince the manager at a store to let you announce over the loud speaker, Honey, this is (your name), and I just wanted to say I love you.

This week say to your spouse *I love you* in a way your spouse will never forget. I know you have said it hundreds of times, but we all need to hear it again and again. *I love you* never grows old, especially when you find an unusual way to say it.

3 Say "I Love You" in an Unforgettable Way

4 ~ How to Give the Ultimate Hug

*T*here are many different kinds of hugs.

There's the *just got off the ship and haven't seen you in so long* spinning hug.

There's the cold, stiff, *please get off me* hug.

Oh, and there's the *hands-low, let's get these clothes off* hug.

A kiss may be just a kiss, but a hug depends on the intention of the hugger.

There's a certain kind of hug that every spouse craves. It's the spontaneous, long, silent, non-sexual, *I just want to melt into you* hug. Do you know it?

The best time for that hug is when it's unexpected, when your spouse is cooking or looking out the window. You walk into the room, gently spin your spouse around, and melt into the corner of his or her neck. There are no words spoken, reasons given, or favors expected in return.

At first, your spouse might not know what to think. His or her first thought might be *what's this about?* Then a few seconds later, *Is everything okay?* Then your spouse will begin to relax once he or she realizes that you're not going to let go and you don't want anything except to be embraced.

If a picture paints a thousand words, then a hug like this speaks volumes.

Hugging is a lost art. Most people hug as a means to an end (foreplay or communication) or to fulfill an obligation. A good hug is complete all by itself. It's the kind of hug that's intimate but not sexual, expressive but not verbal, silent but not cold. I'm talking about the kind of hug that says *you are the center of my universe*.

Find this hug within you and share it with your spouse.

4

Give the Ultimate Hug

5 ~ WHILE NO ONE IS LOOKING

I want to suggest you do something kind, thoughtful, or loving for your spouse. Here's the wrinkle; it has to be something your spouse will NEVER know about.

You're probably thinking *why do something kind for my spouse if he or she won't know about the kindness? I won't get any "points" for it.*

And that's exactly the point.

Search your soul and think about why you do what you do for your spouse? Is it because you want reciprocation? Do you act out of guilt? Do you do it because you feel obligated?

Don't misunderstand. You should do positive things for your spouse and your marriage REGARDLESS of your motivation.

To some extent, alternative motives leave a residue on love. An act of love, by definition, is for the benefit of another. As long as you have even a hint of selfishness, then your gesture is part love and partly a transaction. Your action might be construed as a quid pro quo.

In most spiritual traditions, the highest form of charity is when you give anonymously. When no one knows you gave, that's when you know you gave for the RIGHT reason.

How do you know you're truly a loving spouse? When you do an act of love and your spouse doesn't know you did it. If your spouse doesn't know you did it, you did it for only one reason—because you're a loving spouse!

Give your marriage a boost by extending a gesture of kindness to your spouse without his or her knowledge. Let there be no ulterior motive. Love for one reason and one reason only—because you're loving.

Every relationship is unique and the best idea will be one you think of yourself. Here are a few ideas to get your wheels spinning:

- Fill up your spouse's gas tank.
- Do one of your spouse's chores.

While No One is Looking

- Give your spouse a kiss in the middle of the night.

- Make an anonymous donation in honor of your spouse.

- Plant a tree in honor of your spouse.

- Add an item to your spouse's collection.

- Put a new article of clothing in your spouse's closet.

- Write a poem for your spouse and submit it to an online poem archive.

5 Extend a Kindness—Anonymously

6 ～ How to Win Control

*O*ne of the keys to succeeding in marriage is self-mastery.

Sometimes a client will say to me, *I don't know what came over me. I couldn't control myself...* Then continue:

> *I just kept screaming at him.*
> *I know I shouldn't have spent that money but...*
> *I was scared that if I told the truth then...*
> *I wanted to stop after one drink but...*
> *I know it's not right to check his/her email but...*
> *I promised no more porn sites but...*

There are two parts to you. There's your true self, your soul, which knows what's right and wants to do it. Then there are your instincts, your desires that yearn to be satisfied.

Are you ready for the most important question of life?

Who's in charge? Who rules whom? Is your true self (your soul) the master of your desires, or do your desires dominate you? Do you (the REAL you) decide how you behave or are you overwhelmed by your urges?

A great spouse acts based on his or her values and vision for a loving marriage rather than impulses. A great spouse controls his or her desires.

Self-mastery is the difference between having the relationship you want long term and fulfilling an impulse in the short term.

So how do you develop self-mastery? How do you learn to control your urges and act based on your values and vision rather than your desires? It's simple...PRACTICE.

Self-mastery is a learned skill. Once you get the feel for what it's like to control your desires, you can control them at will.

Pick one desire and practice conquering it. Learn to submit your feelings to your will.

Here are some examples of how you can practice self-mastery.

- Fast for a day.

- Stop smoking for a day.

- Do you feel compelled to exercise every day? Skip a day!

- Do you *have to* watch the news every night? Go on a one-day TV fast.

- Do you bite your nails? Pick a day and don't do it.

You can see that you don't have to pick something you shouldn't be doing. Your assignment is NOT to kick a bad habit (although that's always a good idea). Your assignment is only to practice self-mastery. Obviously, eating is not something you should refrain from everyday. However, fasting for one day can help you develop your ability to conquer your impulses. If you can learn to conquer your impulses and submit your desires to your will, you're on your way to being a better spouse.

6

Demonstrate Self Mastery

7 ~ Sing, Sing a Song...

*D*o you remember singing songs with friends? You're driving along on a road trip, a great song comes on, and you and your friends spontaneously belt it out. Then, as the song winds down, you joke, laugh, or talk. Somehow, it seems like you're better friends after singing together.

You know what's amazing about singing compared to talking? When you talk at the same time, you interrupt each other.

Singing is just the opposite. When two people sing, the whole point is to do it together.

Talking at the same time creates conflict. Singing at the same time creates harmony.

Have you ever been to a rock concert? The band plays the first few notes of its most popular song, everyone screams, flicks their lighter, and starts singing. It feels like you're best friends with 30,000 people, doesn't it?

Something special happens when people sing together. When two people join their voices, it unites their hearts.

Pick a song to sing together. Pick one you really like. If you have it on your iPod, then play it while you sing together. If not, go online, print out the lyrics, and do a home performance. If you're feeling bold, invite your kids to listen. If you're not feeling bold at all, have a drink first.

You might be thinking *I'll pass on this one*. Too awkward, right? Don't skip this one.

It'll be weird at first, but I PROMISE YOU you'll get past that and you'll have fun. Be silly for three minutes together. Sing a song with your spouse.

7 *Sing a Song Together*

8 ~ Why Change is Good

A study once showed that work productivity increased in offices where the lights were dimmed.

However, after a few weeks, productivity returned to the original level. Since the lighting didn't seem to have a long-term impact on productivity, the lighting was returned to its original brightness. Guess what happened? Productivity went up!

What's going on? Is it lower lighting or higher lighting that increases productivity?

Eventually, the study revealed that neither low lighting nor high lighting increased productivity. It was the CHANGE in lighting!

Change stimulates people.

This was never more apparent to me than when we moved to Baltimore after living in Florida for nine years.

Everyone who takes a winter vacation in Florida fantasizes about how wonderful it would be to live in a warm climate. That's because they don't live in a warm climate. After years of only warm weather, many people feel differently.

My wife and I feel more vibrant where we experience the CHANGE of seasons living in the northeast.

I never realized how many things change with the seasons. It's not just the temperature; it's also the sounds, the colors, the taste of the air, and the weight of your clothes. All those changes on the outside stimulate us on the inside.

Don't worry; I'm not advising you to move to Baltimore, and I have nothing against living in Florida. (What matters is not where you live, but what lives within you.) There's no need to pray for climate changes in your area.

The point is to change your environment.

Let's transition from the abstract to the practical. Here are some quick and easy ways to change your environment:

- Light candles throughout your house
- Fill one room in your house with flowers

- Play mood music. Pick music you don't usually listen to and a type that's truly inspiring. Try sounds like Enya, Josh Groban, or classical music.

- Burn incense

You could recycle variations of every one of the above ideas and utilize them periodically. May the changes to your environment stimulate changes in your marriage.

8

Change Your Environment

9 ~ How to Make Memories

*D*o you know the song *Memories* from the movie *The Way We Were* with Robert Redford and Barbra Streisand?

Memories and love go hand-in-hand. When you remember things about your relationship, it says to your spouse *you're important to me.*

Do you remember buying your alarm clock? You probably don't remember because it wasn't an important event.

Do you remember your wedding day? Of course you do.

NORMALLY, the little things we forget and the important things we remember.

But what if I remembered what color shirt you wore when we met five years ago. That's a little thing. However, if I remembered it, you would feel important.

Human nature is to remember what's important. So the SMALLER the things you remember about your spouse and your marriage, the more important your spouse feels.

To boost your marriage, create a *Memories Box* and start saving mementos of your life together. Don't just save things from the big events, include the little ones too. Save tickets from special events, programs from concerts, restaurant receipts, newspapers dated your spouse's birthday, etc.

Keep filling your *Memories Box* and then every once in awhile give a collage, a scrapbook, or a decorative memory box to your spouse. If you want to shed some tears together, put on the song *Memories* before you present it.

9 *Start a "Memories Box"*

10 ~ Pssst...Pass This to My Spouse

*D*o you remember passing notes to your boyfriend/girlfriend in grade school?

Why was it such a thrill to get a note passed to you in class? Because in the back of your mind you're thinking: *With all these people watching...just when they might miss what's going to be on the test...given the risk that they caught and get sent to the principal's office; they are focused on me!?*

In other words, getting a note in class made you feel that your boyfriend or girlfriend blocked out the whole world and for just a moment risked everything to connect with you. No wonder childhood loves are so memorable.

Let's make your adult love memorable. Some things never change. Passing a love note to your spouse in the middle of a holiday dinner or the company banquet will make your spouse burst with a smile just like in junior high school.

Write a sweet love note to your spouse. Fold it up and slip it to your spouse at a table filled with your friends, family, colleagues, or kids. You can do it at a

family dinner or a company outing. The more people around, the more aston-
ished your spouse will be. Watch the grin on your spouse's face and enjoy how
it will transport both of you back to the sweet times of classroom love notes.

10 *Slip Your Spouse a Note*

11 ～ THE SPEED OF MARRIAGE

*A*ll day you run to do this and run to do that.

Slow down. Stop running and take a WALK. I mean it literally. Go for a walk with your spouse.

Normally, when you leave the house with your spouse, you're going somewhere. This time when you leave the house with your spouse, don't go anywhere. Just walk. You're already where you're supposed to be…with your spouse!

Remember that this is not a walk for exercise. It's not a speed walk. If you're one of those people always a few paces ahead of your spouse, concentrate on walking TOGETHER.

The nice thing about going for a walk with your spouse compared to going out to dinner, for example, is that you won't feel pressure to talk. When you're sitting across a table from someone having dinner, you feel like you have to make conversation. Sometimes, however, it feels good to be with someone in silence. A leisurely stroll is conducive to silence.

I took a walk with my wife after writing a draft of this chapter. It was a Sunday afternoon. My kids were in the pool and my wife was reorganizing a room. I printed out a draft of this chapter, took it with me, and said, "Honey, can we go for a short walk?"

"Why," she asked.

"Just because," I responded.

She humored me and we walked. I showed her my favorite house down the street and then I asked her to give me her thoughts on what I wrote. She smiled as she reviewed it and said, "I like it."

I hope you do too.

Take a Walk Together

12 ～ How to Celebrate Your Anniversary Today

*W*hen is your anniversary? Let's say it's November 19. So that's 11/19, right? But for our purposes, let's make it 11:19, as in 11:19 AM. Your assignment is to call your spouse at exactly that time and say, "It's 11:19 and I was thinking about you. Do you know why? Happy anniversary!"

If you did that every day, you could celebrate your anniversary 365 times a year. If you used 11:19 PM too, you could celebrate your anniversary 730 times a year. That might be a bit excessive (even annoying), but once would be cute. Try it.

12 Say "Happy Anniversary"—Today!

13 ~ How to React to Your Spouse

*H*ere's an outline of this chapter:

1. A POWERFUL story

2. An email exchange I had with a new subscriber that illustrates the point of the story.

3. Your assignment is to translate both the story and the email exchange into a practical way to boost your marriage.

Here's the story.

A man once came to a town and asked the local sage, "I'm thinking about moving here. What kind of people live here?"

The sage asked the man, "What kind of people live where you came from?"

"Where I'm from the people are liars, cheaters, and mean spirited," the man responded.

"The people are the same here," said the sage.

Then ANOTHER MAN came to town and asked the sage the same question, "I'm thinking about moving here. What kind of people live here?"

The sage asked the man, "What kind of people live where you came from?"

"Where I'm from the people are wonderful, kind, and courteous," the man responded.

"The people are the same here," said the sage.

People are not as you see them; people are as YOU are.

What do you get when you smile at someone? You get a smile back. The same applies when you stare at someone. They stare back.

What you get is what you are.

We're NOT an objective observer of the people in our life; we're a subjective influence. In other words, our presence changes what we observe.

Here's a simple example. Let's say you wanted to measure the temperature in a small room. You bring a thermometer into the room and wait for a reading. But since your body temperature is 98.6 degrees, the fact that you're in the room changes the reading you get.

It works the same in your marriage. Your relationship is not simply a function of whom you married. It's also a function of who you are.

I offer a free report called *7 Secrets to Fixing Your Marriage* to anyone who signs up at www.MortFertel.com. There's no catch. It's free and there's some very useful marriage advice for anyone who subscribes. (One subscriber even said, "I have learned more about my marriage from your free info than I have from the therapist we've been seeing.") Here's an email exchange I had with a NEW subscriber. I think it proves my point.

The first email I received from her was entitled "Free my rear end," and she wrote as follows:

You put on your website free counseling and then you try to sell me your book. Even if your book was the end all be all, I wouldn't buy it because you already lied. There's nothing free; just 'buy my book. That's hardly the way to build trust in your potential customers. I'm glad your wife likes you. I don't.
    Laurie

Like any normal human being, my first impulse was to write this woman back and give her a piece of my mind. How dare she call me a liar! How dare she question my professional integrity! I had a knee jerk reaction that almost caused me to react to this woman's accusations. But I didn't react because I don't think we should allow others to control our behavior. I didn't want this woman to control who I am, how I behave, or the person I become. Thank you very much, but I'll decide all that for myself. No matter how she treats me, I'm going to be proactive based on my VALUES; not reactive based on her weaknesses. I wrote her back as follows:

Dear Laurie, my apologies for the misunderstanding. In fact, I offer lots of free advice just like I say I do. You can sign up to receive my free report "7 Secrets for Fixing Your Marriage" at www.MortFertel.com. Laurie, not only do I do what I say, but as you'll see if you sign up, I deliver to you (for free) much more than I promised.

Warm regards to you,

Mort Fertel

Nothing fancy. Just pleasant, professional, and to the point. Here's the email I got back from her:

Thanks Mort, I apologize for barking at you. Misdirected anger. It's my husband of 11 years I would like to drop-kick into next week. Anyway, I will look at your stuff and see if any of it applies.

Slightly hopeful,

Laurie

Isn't it amazing how she turned around? I was nice so she was nice back. You only get one guess how she would have reacted had I responded with a nasty email. Instead, I returned her hostility with kindness and got back exactly what I put out. That's what's happening to her in her marriage. She's angry with her husband, and it's her anger that's partly to blame for her husband being the way he is.

When your spouse barks, yells, screams, or complains to you, don't RE-ACT! Instead, gather your strength and respond with love.

I know it's difficult, but you can do it. Don't let your spouse determine what kind of person you will be. Decide now that you're going to be a loving, gentle, compassionate person REGARDLESS of how your spouse treats you. That's power. That's freedom. That's who you want to be.

13 Respond to Anger with Love

14 ~ What you can learn from Winnie the Pooh

*M*y children often ask me to read to them. Day or night, they love to sit on my lap (there are five of them, so it's crowded) or around the table and listen to me read.

It's amazing how the decimal level with five kids can go from unbearable to negligible with the swing of a book cover.

Why and what are my children responding to?

Reading to someone is a completely unselfish act. My children know that when I read to them, that it's for them. Why else would I read Winnie the Pooh?

Your assignment is to read to your spouse (I do not recommend Winnie the Pooh).

Reading aloud to someone is about one thing…connecting. It's about sharing, and I don't mean the sharing of information. It's about sharing time and energy. It's about sharing yourself. Transform your marriage from good to great: read to your spouse.

STEP 1: Choose something to read that will interest your spouse *and* you. If you read a new recipe, but you hate cooking, the experience will come off as plastic. Choose wisely.

STEP 2: Choose the right time. Wait for the right moment. Make sure the kids are asleep. Ask permission first. Say, *there's something I want to read to you. Do you have a moment?* Invite your spouse to sit down. Make sure you're both comfortable. Take your time.

STEP 3: Read aloud. Read slowly. Enjoy.

14 Read Aloud to Your Spouse

15 ~ Time to Rhyme

*T*he word *poem* in the heading may have you thinking, *he's going to ask me to write a love poem*.

Maybe next time.

If I'm going to take you into the world of poetry, then I want the poem to have the greatest possible impact on your marriage.

But Mort, what could be more wonderful than for us to write love poems to each other?

For thousands of years, people have been pouring out their hearts to each other in poetry. It's beautiful. Don't let me hold you back. Go ahead and write a love poem if you want. However, there's a poem you can write that will do more for your marriage than any love poem you could write for your spouse. That poem is a poem you write together!

Think about when someone writes a love poem to his or her beloved. Who has the most powerful experience, the one who writes the poem or the one who receives it? Who feels the most inside? Who's most inspired? Who feels the most love? Yes, you got it. It's the person who *writes* the poem. That's why I want you to write a poem together.

Writing a poem is a unique experience. Once you get into it, IT is all there is. When you're absorbed in rhyming verses and sharing feelings, all your worries fade away. When there are just your words and thoughts and your effort to coordinate the two, you're immersed in the moment. There's no regretful past and no anxiety about the future. When you're in the midst of composing a poem, there's never anywhere to go. Writing a poem is like creating an island of focus.

Focus. That's the hard part about spending time together. Someone is always distracted. Someone always has something on his or her mind, a deadline to meet, a program to watch, a phone to answer, or an appointment. What about just being together? Couples share so much - a house, money, kids, furniture, cars, etc. The one thing couples don't share enough of is time. Yet that's where relationships blossom.

Time to Rhyme

Writing a poem together is about delving into time together. It's about being together without distractions. It's an experience, by its very nature, that excludes worries, anxieties, problems, activities, appointments, and other people.

So what's the topic of your poem?

Poems are great for all occasions. My wife and I wrote a poem to our son for his eighth birthday. Write a poem to someone for an upcoming graduation or anniversary. Do you have a family celebration, holiday dinner, July 4th picnic, or religious occasion coming up? Write a poem for it. You can make it funny, touching, or both. Your poem will be well received if it rhymes and if you're sincere.

The nice thing about this exercise is that you don't have to be on any particular terms with your spouse to do it. In fact, it's a great excuse for connecting if things aren't going great. *Joey's birthday is coming up. I know he'd feel really good if we honored him with a poem during his party. Will you help me write it one night this week?*

Don't worry about quality. It doesn't have to be a good poem. You don't need any experience. Just have fun.

To prove that you don't need any special talent, here's the poem my wife and I composed for our son:

HAPPY BIRTHDAY ZACHARIAH

On July 30, eight years ago,
you came into our lives and made us glow.

We started asking ourselves right away,
"How do we raise him in a good way?"

Time to Rhyme

But within no time we could see,
that God blessed you tremendously.

You were good at things before we even taught,
You always knew to do just as you ought.

Your goodness comes from a place deep within,
It's amazing to see how you're always tuned-in.

You laugh when there's fun and cry when it hurts,
You love to sing and do you remember dancing to Mary Poppins and Bert?

Whether it's Legos, Playmobile, a set-up, or blocks,
Your creativity is absolutely tops.

Your love for animals whether it's fish, frogs, or bugs,
Just shows that you, Zachariah, are like a giant hug!

We love you, we're proud, you bring us such joy,
You really are such a wonderful boy.

You love to snuggle, cuddle, and sit on our lap,
Your love simply has no gap.

So happy birthday to you our son,
Your Mommy and Daddy will always love you a ton.

And last but not least our wish for you,
Is that the spark of God keeps shining through you.

Love, Mommy and Daddy

TIME TO RHYME

Take time with your spouse to write a poem. Find a reason or pick an occasion and work on it together.

I wish you luck that you find the right theme,
That you and your spouse can be a team.

Don't worry if your poem is good or not,
Just make some rhymes and at the end put a dot.

Sit down with each other and forget the rest,
I have confidence you can pass this test.

As you start to compose line after line,
I know more and more you'll enjoy your time.

So until next time, I hope you stay well,
I'll be in the next chapter, with another exercise to tell.

15 Compose a Poem Together

16 ~ It's All in Your Hands

*L*ook at your hands. Go ahead. Stop reading this now and take a good look at your hands.

I'll get back to your hands in a moment.

My wife and I went one weekend to Harve de Grace, MD, a quaint old town, and stayed in a small two-story cottage. It was one of our quarterly romantic retreats.

One day, while we strolled through the tree-lined streets admiring the old Victorian inns, we passed an outdoor wedding. The aisle for the bride and groom started at the sidewalk and ended at the wedding canopy fifty feet from the street. We happened to walk by as the ceremony began. I, of course, was interested in what the pastor would say to the young bride and groom.

Wedding ceremonies are a time for idealism not realism, so I wasn't expecting to hear profound words from the pastor. But to my surprise, she led the bride and groom through a meaningful exercise and offered them sound advice. I'm going to use my own words, but here's essentially what happened.

The pastor acknowledged that brides and grooms usually gaze into each other's eyes with heartfelt emotion (she paused to notice that that's exactly what the bride and groom in front of her were doing). She spoke about the innocence of that look and the sea of feelings shared without a word spoken. Then the pastor kindly asked the bride and groom to bow their heads and look at their hands.

It's amazing how the energy in a place can shift in a moment. When the bride and groom turned their attention from each other's eyes to their hands, it was as though the pastor had transported them from a fairytale to a drama. Then the pastor explained as follows.

You decided to spend the rest of your lives together because of your feelings, but the rest of your lives together will be decided by your actions.

"Take a good look at your hands," the pastor requested of the bride and groom. *Because it's what you DO for the next fifty years that will determine what you see in each other's eyes.*

It's All in Your Hands

In other words, what you see is *not* what you get. What you *do* is what you will see.

We all want to gaze into our spouse's eyes and feel the depth of their love. But in the long term, those looks are not because we met Mr. or Ms. Right. It's because we did RIGHT and because we earned the right over time to see that love reflected in our spouse's eyes.

Look at your hands again. Remember your wedding vows? Remember that look in your spouse's eyes? What are you going to do this week so you can see that love? Commit to at least one gesture and fulfill your commitment.

16 Extend an Act of Kindness

17 — THAT'S A GOOD ONE

A lot of people when asked why they fell in love will say, *because he/ she made me laugh*.

When two people talk at the same time, it usually means they're fighting. But when two people laugh at the same time, it means they're uniting.

We don't laugh with everyone. It takes a willingness to be childlike. You have to be ready to let your hair down. Oh sure, we'll politely laugh with anyone, but an uninhibited laugh together, it's an intimate experience.

Most courtships are filled with jokes, fun, and laughter. However, in marriage, jokes, fun and laughter are replaced quickly by chores, responsibility, and financial obligations.

How about a laugh with your spouse this week? Trust me; it will be good for your marriage.

Tell your spouse a good joke or otherwise have a laugh together. Ask around at the office or do some online research, but one way or another find a good joke. Here's one you can use:

A guy takes his wife to her first football game. They had great seats right behind their team's bench. After the game, he asked her how she liked the experience.

"Oh, I really liked it," she replied, "especially the tight pants and the big muscles, but I couldn't understand why they were killing each other over 25 cents."

Dumbfounded, her husband asked, "What do you mean?"

"Well, they flipped a coin, one team got it and then for the rest of the game, all they kept screaming was: 'Get the quarterback! Get the quarterback!' I'm like . . . Hel-loooooo? It's only 25 cents!!!!

17 *Tell Your Spouse a Joke*

*D*id you ever think about why people love sports?

I remember I had a session with a husband who had a marital crisis. One of the questions I asked in an effort to diagnose his situation was "What's most important to you in order of priority?" He said 1) softball, 2) his friends, and 3) his family.

It turns out that number one and two were related because he loved the camaraderie with the guys on his softball team.

His priorities certainly reflect his crisis, but the connection he cultivates with the guys on his softball team is real. It's reflective of a dynamic that you can use to improve your marriage.

Couples who play together stay together.

The real joy of being on a team is not winning; it's connecting.

Play with your spouse to try to connect all the dots below using four *straight* lines *without* lifting your pen off the paper.

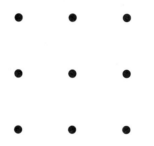

Solution: www.MortFertel.com/good-to-great-18.asp

Play a Game Together

19 ～ Brain Teasers for Two

*P*roblems are opportunities for your marriage. The key is teamwork. When a couple becomes a team and deals with problems together, rather than dividing responsibility or pointing the finger, then the marriage improves. I can't make any promises about whether the problem gets resolved, but if you work on it together, your marriage will be better off.

Here are some problems for you to work on together. We'll call them brain teasers.

Here's the first one:

    MAN
    BOARD

That's *man overboard*. Get it?

How about this one:

R/E/A/D/I/N/G

That's *reading between the lines.*

Okay, now the rest are for you and your spouse to grapple with.

WEAR
LONG

Here's another:

MIND
MATTER

And another:

> HE'S / HIMSELF

Let's not stop now:

> DEATH LIFE

Last one:

> KNEE
> ———
> LIGHT

For the answers to these brain teasers, go to www.MortFertel.com/brain-teasers.asp.

19

Solve a Problem Together

20 ∼ Make it a 5-Star Night

*H*ave you ever been to a 5-star hotel?

One of the special experiences of a 5-star hotel is that the staff turns down your bed and puts a piece of chocolate on your pillow. That careful attention to your comfort makes the hotel 5-star.

Most of us don't go to 5-star hotels too often, but why not give your spouse 5-star attention at home? It's so easy. Just turn down your spouse's side of the bed and put a piece of chocolate on the pillow. Don't forget the slippers below the edge of the bed.

This assignment should take about fifteen seconds, but it's one of those gestures that says *I'm thinking about your comfort. I'm thinking about you.* Give it a try.

Give 5-Star Treatment

21 ~ How to Replace Efficiency with Intimacy

*D*o you know Henry Ford's greatest accomplishment? It wasn't inventing the automobile. Henry Ford did *not* invent the automobile. What he invented was a revolutionary way to mass-produce the automobile. Henry Ford perfected the assembly line. He understood division of labor, and division of labor has been the model of efficiency ever since the Model T. Divide and conquer . . . that's the ticket, right?

Division of labor will serve you well at work, but not at home.

The chances are that you and your spouse have a lot of chores and responsibilities. The most efficient way to get them done is to divide and conquer. Efficiency is the goal in the office, but not in your home. When it comes to your marriage, the secret is not efficiency; it's intimacy!

Think about the terminology "*division* of labor" and "*divide* and conquer." That's exactly what will happen to you and your spouse. You'll be divided. To succeed in marriage, however, you want to be united.

To help take your marriage from good to great, do a chore together.

I know you don't need help. I know it's faster and easier to do it alone, but then you'll be alone. Do it together, not because the task will be done better, but because your marriage will be better.

If you usually make dinner, ask your spouse to help you in the kitchen. And make it fun!

If it's your job to pick the kids up after school, ask your spouse to join you for the ride.

If you plan to fold the laundry tonight, why not ask your spouse to help. Don't ask your spouse to do it. Ask your spouse to help.

Or join your spouse while he or she is doing a chore.

Does your spouse water the plants? Grab another pitcher and water the plants together.

Is your spouse the resident handyman? Grab a tool and pitch in.

Remember, when it comes to your marriage, the secret is not efficiency, it's intimacy!

21 Do a Chore Together

22 ～ Voila—A New You

*A*braham Joshua Heschel said:

"A person is what he aspires for. In order to know myself, I ask: What are the ends I am striving to attain? What are the values I care for most?"

Normally, we think a person is as he or she acts. If a person acts a certain way, then those actions define that person. If a person loses his or her temper, that person is considered a hothead. If a person gives for no particular reason, that person is considered generous. Our actions define us, right?

If we want to be a different person, we usually think we have to behave differently.

In short, conventional wisdom says you are what you do. That's true to a large extent.

However, Heschel, in his statement above, asserts that we are what we want to be. Do you want to be patient? If so, then you just became more patient. Do you want to be sensitive? If so, you just became more sensitive.

Your vision for yourself, to some extent, defines who you are even before you realize that vision.

Did you ever meet someone with big dreams? Somehow, the dreams define that person . . . even before the dreams come true.

Every day I meet people who had a wakeup call and are determined to become better spouses. The only thing that's really changed is their conviction. If you talked to them like I do, you would feel that to some extent they're a better spouse already simply because they have new expectations for themselves.

Your assignment is to pick one thing you want to be different about you and announce it.

Do you want to help around the house more often? Tell your spouse that that's who you want to be.

Do you want to be more physically affectionate? Let your spouse know your intentions.

Aspire to one change in your life. What you aspire for says a lot about who you are even before you fulfill your aspiration.

22 *Announce an Aspiration*

23 ～ How to get Dressed for Your Spouse

*E*very morning you go to your closet, think about what you feel like wearing, and get dressed. What you wear is based most likely on how you're feeling, your plans for the day, and the weather forecast. Your marriage probably doesn't factor into your dressing decisions.

For one day this week, consider your spouse when you're getting dressed. What does your spouse like you to wear? What's your spouse's favorite color? What about wearing the sweater your spouse bought for you? Does your spouse like when you wear a particular shirt with a certain pair of pants? Do you remember which undergarments you wore on your last romantic anniversary? Does your spouse have a favorite dress or tie for you to wear?

Get dressed with your spouse in mind and, if your spouse will appreciate it, let your spouse know that you did so.

Seems like a little thing, doesn't it? In some ways it's little, but in other ways it's huge.

Most people have self at the center of their consciousness. We mostly decide what to wear or how to spend an evening based on our own wants. The key, though, to succeeding in a lasting marriage is to shift the center of consciousness from you (as a single entity) to us (as a couple).

This takes rewiring. Who's accustomed to having a *we* perspective? After all, we spent the first 20-30 years of our lives thinking only of ourselves.

Moving from *me to we* requires a rewiring...a completely new perspective. This takes time. You can't do it in a single bound. In the words of Og Mandino, "All great feats are accomplished one small step at a time." So when you step into your clothes next, take a small step for your marriage.

23 *Wear Your Spouse's Favorite*

24 ~ Darling, You Look Marvelous

*T*he last chapter discussed picking your clothes with your spouse in mind.

This time, I want you to turn your attention to *your spouse's* clothes.

Think about what you like your spouse to wear. What color does your spouse look best in? Don't you just love it when your spouse wears…?

Ask your spouse to wear something for you. Why? Because it demonstrates that you care, and that you're thinking about and connected to your spouse.

Honey, why don't you wear that blue shirt today that you look so nice in?

Can you wear your yellow sundress today?

I love the way you look in the v-neck you got for your birthday last year. Why don't you wear that to the party tonight?

You haven't worn that silky lingerie in a while. Do you feel like wearing it tonight?

Asking your spouse to wear something for you demonstrates that you're tuned into your spouse and that what he or she does matters to you. It shows that you care about the details of your spouse's life. It's a sign that you're connected, even to the clothes on your spouse's back. It's just a simple way to say, *I notice you*.

24 *Ask for Your Favorite...*

25 ~ Ooh La La

*T*here's a special bond that parents feel when they tend to the physical needs of their child. For example, I loved it when my four years olds (we're blessed with triplets) came to me and said, "Daddy, could you button my shirt?"

I feel a special connection with my daughter when I blow dry her hair.

It's particularly special when one spouse cares for another because, unlike the parent-child dynamic, it's not necessary. In other words, your spouse can shave himself. The only reason you're taking the time to shave him is to make a connection...to be intimate.

Shaving your spouse's beard (or her legs) is just one example. Here are some other possibilities:

- button your spouse's shirt

- cut your spouse's toenails

- feed your spouse dessert

- help your spouse on with his or her coat
- brush your spouse's hair
- tie your spouse's shoes
- brush the lint off your spouse's shoulders
- take your spouse's shoes off

Pick one of the above ways to care for your spouse, or choose one of your own ideas.

You can put a lot of love into buttoning a shirt. For example, do it slowly. As you go from button to button, rub the back of your hands against your spouse's chest. If you see a hanging thread, bite it off gently with your teeth.

25 Button Your Spouse's Shirt

*T*here are many famous aphorisms about love and marriage. Here are a few you might appreciate.

"Grief can take care of itself, but to get the full value of joy, you must have somebody to divide it with." — MARK TWAIN

"No man is truly married until he understands every word his wife is NOT saying." — UNKNOWN

"The one thing we can never get enough of is love. And the one thing we never give enough is love." — HENRY MILLER

"All's fair in love and war." — FRANCIS EDWARD SMEDLEY

"One word frees us of all the weight and pain in life. That word is love."
— Sophocles

"Love is an irresistible desire to be irresistibly desired." — Robert Frost

"If I can stop one heart from breaking, I shall not live in vain."
— Emily Dickinson

Some of the above may have struck a chord with you. That's the way it is with old adages. Sometimes we read it and say, *yes, that's so true!* Other times we read them and say, *what in the world does that mean?* Maybe it just falls flat for us and has no special meaning.

All's Fair in Love and War

Your assignment is to find the perfect aphorism for your spouse. Find one that you know will resonate with him or her. Then print it out, write it in a card, or email it to your spouse with a short note, *thought you'd appreciate this* or *thinking of you.*

The key is to find the right quote...the one with which your spouse will connect. You want your spouse to read it and think, *yes, that's perfect for us.*

You can do this regardless of your marital state.

Is your marriage on the rocks? Find a quote about the struggle of love.

Is your marriage going through a passionate stage? Find a quote about the magic of passion.

Are you newlyweds? This should be easy for you.

Every situation is unique. At this moment, there is just the right aphorism waiting for you to discover and share with your spouse.

Where can you find quotes about love and marriage? Take a trip to your local bookstore. There are many books about love and marriage, which include fascinating quotes. Or, Google for what you're looking for.

I hope you find just the right one and I hope your spouse is touched by your effort.

26 Find the Perfect Aphorism

27 ~ The Power of Again

*I*f you sent a gift to me, what would I do after I opened it? I would phone you to say *thank you*. You might think that my thank you is an expression of appreciation.

But that's not necessarily true.

Maybe I'm appreciative for the gift and maybe I'm not. You wouldn't know because I called to say *thank you*. All you would know is that my mother raised me well and that I have good manners. After all, it would be rude to not *thank you*.

What if I called *again* a week later and said *you know that blue shirt you sent me for my birthday? I'm wearing it now and it looks great with the tie my wife bought me. Thank you.*

Why did I call you that second time?

It could only be because I'm thankful.

The first *thank you* could be obligation. The second *thank you* could only be appreciation.

I have two ideas for you. First, think of something your spouse did last week that you could express appreciation for again. Either verbally or in writing say, *thank you*.

Second, make a list of things your spouse does this week for which you expressed appreciation and make a note to remind yourself to say *thank you* again next week.

As is often the case, this would be a great habit. I encourage you to make a mental note (or keep a list) of things your spouse does that deserves appreciation and occasionally come back to your list. Remember them! Remember to say *thank you* again.

27 *Say "Thank You" Again.*

28 ~ EFFECTIVE AFFECTION

*E*veryone shows affection in his or her own way. Likewise, everyone likes to be shown affection in a certain way. The question is do you show affection in the way your spouse likes to be shown? In other words, do you show your affection effectively?

If your spouse needs physical affection, but you give only verbal affirmation, you'll have problems.

Expressing affection is a form of communication. The first rule of communication is to speak in the language your spouse understands.

If your spouse understands touch, then touch. If your spouse understands poems, then write poems. If your spouse understands gifts, then give gifts.

This is also a challenge for parents. We have so much wisdom to offer our children, but how do we impart our wisdom to a five year old, a fifteen year old, or a thirty year old?

As the years go by, parents have to be able to adjust the way they teach their children to accommodate their changing capacity to learn.

In order to express your affection effectively in your marriage, you have to modify your method of communication to match your spouse's needs.

a. List the two primary ways you show affection.

1. _____

2. _____

b. How does your spouse want you to show affection?

1. _____

2. _____

c. Compare your findings from questions *a* and *b* on the previous page.

d. Express affection effectively at least twice this week by demonstrating your affection in exactly the way your spouse prefers.

29 — How to Heal Old Wounds

*F*ind a piece of paper. Before you read on, please get a piece of paper. Now, stretch out your arm straight ahead and hold that paper. Are you holding it up? What do you guess it weighs?

Keep holding the paper. Don't put it down yet.

As you continue to hold the paper, you'll notice that its weight doesn't matter as much as how long you hold it. The longer you hold that piece of paper, the heavier it feels. Eventually, your arm will tire and that little piece of paper will feel as though it weighs as much as a ton of bricks.

It works the same in your marriage. Hurts will happen between you and your spouse that will weigh heavily on your heart. The longer you hold onto hurt, the heavier the burden feels.

On many occasions in private sessions I'll discover that the source of someone's anger or bitterness is something that happened fifteen years ago!

"Did you ever discuss what happened with your spouse," I'll ask.

"No," is the response.

In an effort to make sure I understand, I'll ask, "You never talked it through? You never processed with your spouse at all?"

"No," is the response.

Rhetorically I'll ask, "This has been building up inside you for fifteen years and you never said anything?"

"That's right," is the response.

Do you hear that? It happened fifteen years ago! It still hurts. In fact, as I illustrated above, the burden gets heavier the longer you hold on to it.

What have you been holding on to? Think about it because it's not healthy and the burden only gets worse.

Most of us have something that continues to bother us, something that happened years ago that we never let go, or something that we never moved through with our spouse. There it sits, getting heavier and heavier as the years go by.

If there's something in your past that burdens you, try to talk through it.

It might not be a fun talk. It might be painful. Your spouse might feel that you're bringing up old wounds. But old wounds that aren't treated aren't old. They're fresh. They're open sores, and they worsen over time. Let it go. Put the paper down.

29

Clear the Air

30 ~ Do the Right Thing

People are often unreasonable, illogical, and self-centered:
Forgive them anyway.
If you are kind, people may accuse you of selfish, ulterior motives;
be kind anyway.
If you are honest and frank, people may cheat you;
be honest and frank anyway.
What you spend years building, someone could destroy overnight;
build anyway.
If you find serenity and happiness, they may be jealous;
be happy anyway.
The good you do today, people will often forget tomorrow;
do good anyway.
Give the world your best anyway.
You see, in the final analysis, it is between you and God;
it was never between you and them anyway.

— Mother Teresa

Share the above quote with your spouse. It's about having the right intention. It's about being driven by an inner compass that's not affected by outside circumstances. It's about your actions being accountable to the only real Judge.

Find one action in your marriage you're withholding because of your spouse or some other outside circumstance. Then do it! Don't hold back. Do it because it's the right thing to do. Do it because you know the only real Judge will judge you favorably.

Don't Hold Back

31 ~ Are You Packed Properly?

*I*f you were taking a trip tomorrow, what would you pack?

Oh, you need to know where you're going before you can pack. You make a good point!

You pack differently if you go to Florida than if you go to Iceland. How can you pack until you know where you're going?

It's the same with your marriage. How can you plan your week as a spouse unless you first decide where you want your marriage to go?

If you decide you want your marriage to include time together this week, then it's obvious you need to plan date night. If you decide you want your marriage this week to include one random act of kindness, then you can plan an unexplained gesture of kindness.

The key is to know first where you're going. What do you want your marriage to look like this week?

Think about where you want your marriage to go this week, then decide on one corresponding action that will help you get there.

For example, if you want your marriage to include romance this week, you might plan a candlelit slow dance in the living room. Maybe you want your marriage to include more order this week. If so, plan to organize your bills together.

Where is your marriage going this week? Decide and start packing.

31 *Make a Weekly Marriage Plan*

32 ⁓ How to Create a Moment of Joy

I learned something from my son that I want to share with you and suggest you apply it in your marriage.

We were sitting on the couch reading a book. Part way through the book I said, "You know, this is a really good book."

My son replied, "Daddy, you bought me this book when we went to Barnes and Noble together."

"I did?" I asked, not remembering.

"Yes," he said, assuring me that I deserved the credit.

I felt good at that moment. It made me happy that my son remembered that I bought him the book. I felt good about being at least partially responsible for us enjoying the book together.

Get enjoyment from something your spouse gave you and then remind your spouse that he or she gave it to you.

This is a simple gesture. However, if you give your spouse a fraction of the joy my son gave to me, it will be a winning moment for both of you and for your marriage.

Give Your Spouse Joy

33 ~ CLOSE TO YOUR HEART

*O*n page 93 of *Marriage Fitness*, I discuss the Photo Op. If you have read *Marriage Fitness*, you may remember that I recommend surrounding yourself with photos of your spouse. I suggest putting pictures of your spouse in your wallet, your office, your locker, on your desk, etc.

One day my wife showed me a new silver locket she wore around her neck. It hung close to her heart. I'm not into jewelry, so I responded, "Oh, that's nice. I like it."

But then she opened it and inside was a photo of me next to her heart!

We smiled at each other, locked eyes, and had a nice moment together. I was touched.

It was one of those sweet, thoughtful gestures. That simple (and loving) gesture made my day special and memorable.

If you're a woman, buy yourself a necklace locket that opens and put a photo of your husband inside. You don't have to spend a lot of money; just enough to get something you'll enjoy wearing. Then show it to your husband and ask him if he wants to see what's inside. Watch his eyes when you open it up and show him that his photo hangs next to your heart.

If you're a man, buy a necklace locket for your wife and put your photo or a photo of the two of you inside.

33 *Buy a Locket & Add a Photo*

34 ~ Just Say No

ihaly Csikszentmihalyi (don't worry, I can't pronounce it ei-ther), a modern psychologist and author, wrote a fascinating book called "Creativity: Flow and the Psychology of Discovery and Invention."

In preparation for writing the book, Professor Csikszentmihalyi inter-viewed over a hundred of the most creative people in the world including historians, composers, poets, artists, writers, scientists, economists, inven-tors, and business leaders. In order to get over a hundred of the most creative people in the world to agree to participate in his study, he had to send out a few hundred invitations.

I want to share with you the response he got from one of the invitees, Peter Drucker, the management expert and professor of Oriental art. He wrote:

"I am greatly honored and flattered by your kind letter of February 14 — for I have admired you and your work for many years, and I have learned much from it. But, my dear Professor Csikszentmihalyi, I am afraid I have

to disappoint you. I could not possibly answer your questions. I am told I am creative—I don't know what that means...I just keep plodding...I hope you will not think me presumptuous or rude if I say that one of the secrets of productivity (in which I believe whereas I do not believe in creativity) is to have a VERY BIG waste paper basket to take care of ALL the invitations such as yours—productivity in my experience consists of NOT doing anything that helps the work of other people but to spend all one's time on the work the Good Lord has fitted one to do, and to do it well."

I'm intrigued by Professor Drucker's approach toward creativity and appalled by his unwillingness to do anything for anyone else. However, there is something we can learn about marriage from his attitudes.

In her book "Lucky in Love: The Secrets of Happy Couples and How Their Marriages Thrive," Catherine Johnson, Ph.D. quotes a clergyman:

Just Say No

"If there were more solid relationships between the husbands and wives in my congregation, we'd have a hard time keeping this church organized as well as it is. If the men and women were mated the way they ought to be, if their lives were full and their hearts full of each other, they would want to be together—and all those evening committee meetings and groups would dwindle to nothing . . . they come here just to work out their desertions at home by these binges of altruism."

Catherine Johnson explains that successfully married couples were often thought of in their community as "odd" and standoffish. People couldn't understand why they weren't social or involved with community events. But in her research, Catherine Johnson discovered that it was because they wanted to be together. It's not that they were saying *no* to social invitations; they were saying *yes* to each other.

That's what Peter Drucker said to Mihaly Csikszentmihalyi in the note I shared with you. Peter Drucker had a burning *yes* for his work and that's why he said *no* to Mihaly Csikszentmihalyi.

As I said, I'm appalled at Peter Drucker's attitude toward helping others, but I think it behooves us to have a burning *yes* for our marriage that motivates us to say *no* sometimes to other invitations.

Your assignment this week is to say *no* to someone or something you would normally say *yes* to and channel that time and energy into your marriage.

You might say *no* to your boss, your child, your mother, a friend, or the head of a committee, but say *no*. And remember, saying *no* is not a negative statement about that relationship. It's a testimony of love for your spouse.

34 *Clear Your Schedule*

35 ～ How to Puzzle Your Way to Clarity

*I*n a recent study, it was discovered that people pondering a complex decision and then stopping to build a puzzle made more satisfying choices than those who deliberated continuously.

Let's talk about why and see how we can use this information to improve your marriage.

There are two different modes or styles of thinking:

1. Intuitive, creative, right-brain thinking
2. Logical, linear, left brain thinking

Most people are either left-brain thinkers or right-brain thinkers. Most people either go with their gut or analyze heavily.

Think about you and your spouse. The chances are good that one of you explains your decisions and makes perfect sense while the other decides apparently without thinking.

Left-brain linear thinkers become accountants and engineers. Right-brain creative thinkers become artists, social workers, and human resource consultants.

Most people feel their way of thinking is right, but both are right for different situations. If you're trying to solve a math problem, then you want to go with your left (logical). If you're trying to resolve a dispute between your children, then you want to go with your right (creative).

When we face a decision, most of us bring to bear our natural mode of thinking. In other words, if we're a predominant left-brain thinker, we'll analyze every decision. I know people who decided who to marry using a checklist. On the other hand, other people blatantly ignored important facts.

The truth is, although some decisions are best suited for a logical analysis while others for a creative process, all decisions can benefit from left and right-brain thought processes.

How to Puzzle Your Way to Clarity

That's why building a puzzle can help you make a wise decision. When building a puzzle, you first plan. You work on the edges or a particular color. You have to establish some order, some structure. Once only the center is left to complete, finishing the puzzle requires intuition. Building a puzzle forces you to use both halves of your brain.

In a marriage, there's usually one person who is more intuitive and one who is more logical. Usually, people have a tough time relating to each other's modes of thinking. The truth is that family decisions are served the best when each spouse brings his or her method of thinking to bear on the decision and creates a space for his or her spouse to use the opposite method of thinking.

That's the beauty of marriage. Between the two of you, you can come from the left and from the right and give every decision a complete look.

Your assignment for this week: Get a puzzle! The next time you and your spouse face a decision, build it together, and then decide using both of your thinking styles.

he following might make you a little squeamish, but I think my point will make it worthwhile.

Daniel Kahneman, a professor of psychology at Princeton University, did a fascinating psychological study using the technique of colonoscopy.

A colonoscopy is where the scope on a tube is inserted into the rectum and moved up and down the bowels so the innards can be viewed. Needless to say, a colonoscopy is quite uncomfortable and the time it takes seems like eternity (even though it only takes a few minutes).

In one of Kahneman's experiments, 682 patients were randomly assigned to the usual colonoscopy or to a procedure in which one extra minute was added at the end. In the case of the second group who had to endure an extra minute, the colon scope did not move at all during that extra minute.

Obviously, it's not nearly as uncomfortable when the colon scope isn't moving around. However, this second group had to endure an extra minute, which means that they experienced greater overall pain. Since their last minute was relatively less uncomfortable, their memory of the entire ordeal was not as bad as the group who actually endured the procedure for one minute less. In fact, the second group, who endured the scope in the rectum for longer, was *more willing* to go through the procedure again.

What's the point and how does this relate to your marriage?

Endings are important. Pay attention to them.

How does your morning end with your spouse? Do you say goodbye and hug before you part for the day?

What about your phone conversations? How do they end? Do you just hang up or is there an exchange of pleasantries?

How does dinner end in your home? Does everyone just get up from the table and leave or does everyone help clean up and thank the cook?

How does your day end? Do you just fall asleep on the couch watching TV or do you design a healthy end to your day together with a drink, a talk, love making, or a kiss goodnight?

What you can learn from a Pain in the Butt

Pick one facet of your relationship (the morning, phone calls, dinnertime, bedtime, whatever) and focus on creating a healthier ending. End one facet of your relationship this week on a high note, whether it's a hug, a kiss, a wink, a love name, or a joke.

36 Improve Your Endings

37 ~ YOUR GRATITUDE JOURNAL

*I*n his landmark work, *Authentic Happiness*, Martin Seligman, Ph.D. explains that one of the seminal characteristics of a happy person is that they highlight the positive of life.

One of Dr. Seligman's main points is that happiness is not a function of how many good things (or bad things) happen to you nor is it a function of the magnitude of them. Instead, it's a function of the degree to which you recognize and remember them.

In other words, it's not what happens to you; it's what you notice and what you remember. Happy people recognize the goodness in their lives and think of that goodness often.

Unfulfilled people overlook the positive and fail to recall the events they appreciated.

Dr. Seligman's teaching is applicable to your marriage. People who are happy in their marriage *notice and recall* the goodness in their spouse and the blessings that their marriage brings them.

Your assignment is to use a "Gratitude Journal." You can use a simple yellow pad or invest in a nice leather bound piece. In your journal, write down every night at least one thing in your marriage for which you're thankful. Every night, make a note about one good thing your spouse did or one blessing your marriage bestowed upon you.

Also, each night take a moment to read previous entries in your journal and recall positive experiences of the past.

37 Begin a Gratitude Journal

*P*DA: Public Displays of Affection

Why do lovers display their affection publicly? Part of it, of course, is that they simply can't keep their hands off each other.

There's another factor.

The fact that other people are watching contributes something positive to the relationship. It's as if the lovers are saying, *not only do I want to show you how much I love you, but I want to show everyone else too!*

Don't worry. I'm not going to suggest that you display your physical affection publicly. I have my own feelings about the appropriateness of what's commonly accepted.

What I will suggest, however, is that you publicly display your *appreciation*. It's still a PDA, but the "A" stands for appreciation, not affection.

The possibilities about how to do this are endless. Your assignment is to find a way that works for your situation. Here are some examples.

Let's say your husband fixed the bathroom sink. In addition to the good deed, it saved the family $150. You might buy a balloon for each of your children to tie to their chair before dinner, and then sing, "For he's a jolly good fellow…"

Let's say your wife took the kids to an amusement park while you were on your business trip. You don't usually travel and you were concerned about how your youngest child would fare with you gone for a few days. When you returned, they couldn't wait to tell you about the good time they had with mommy at the amusement park.

Later that night while you and your wife are out with friends, you might order a bottle of wine, get everyone's attention, and make a toast to *the most wonderful mother* (and wife) *in the world*.

Public displays of appreciation are not substitutes for expressing yourself privately. PDAs are an add-on that will shine light on your marriage and give a boost to the way you and your spouse feel about each other.

38 Express Appreciation Publicly

39 ～ You Blew It! It's Okay. I'll Love You Anyway.

*I*n Genesis, in the beginning of the Bible, God asks Adam and Eve not to eat from the tree of knowledge of good and evil. After tempted by the serpent, Adam and Eve disobey God and eat from the tree.

Yup, they blew it.

Of course, your spouse blows it sometimes too.

We can learn a lot about how to conduct ourselves in our marriage when our spouse blows it by how God treated Adam and Eve after their blunder.

Do you know what He does? He realizes what they need and He gives it to them.

After Adam and Eve disobey God, they realize they're naked and they feel embarrassed. God sees that they're embarrassed so he gives them clothing.

He gives them clothing? Shouldn't He let them suffer the consequences of their choice? Isn't He condoning their behavior by continuing to care for them? Let them be embarrassed, right?

No.

Love gives. Period!

Loving someone means taking care of the person, giving the person what he or she needs, whether he or she deserves it or not. In fact, it's that kind of unconditional giving and caring that prevents a single mistake in a marriage from spiraling out of control and leading to more mistakes.

Usually, when one spouse blows it, the other spouse uses that as justification to blow it too. Of course, that only makes matters worse.

But imagine if every time your spouse made a mistake, you tended to the need that was created by that mistake.

For example, let's say you ask your spouse not to leave the sewing box at the top of the basement steps because if it is knocked down it will empty and make a big mess. Let's say your spouse ignores you and does it anyway and then your dog knocks the sewing box down the basement steps.

What does your spouse need now?

You Blew It! It's Okay. I'll Love You Anyway.

Your spouse would need two things:

1. Help cleaning up the sewing box pieces
2. Relief from feeling stupid and wrong

Most spouses would say, *I told you not to...*, and leave their spouse to clean up the mess, essentially allowing him or her to suffer the practical and emotional consequences of their mistake. This, of course, makes matters worse between husband and wife and begins the downward spiral.

Why not be more like God was with Adam and Eve? It's true your spouse blew it, but that created needs that you can now fulfill. You might say to your spouse, *I told that dog to stay away from the sewing box* (shifting the blame to the dog and relieving your spouse's emotional guilt), followed by offering your help to clean up (relieving your spouse's practical burden).

There's no doubt that giving your spouse what your spouse needs in the face of his or her mistake is a difficult choice for you to make, but consider the difference it would make in your marriage.

When your spouse makes his or her next mistake (that won't take long, right?), instead of letting your spouse suffer the consequences, step in to ease his or her pain. Whatever needs your spouse might have because of his or her mistake, take care of it. Be like God. I know it's a tall task, but you can do it and it will make a heaven's worth of difference in your marriage.

39 *Let Your Spouse off the Hook*

40 ～ How to Finish Your Spouse's Sentence

*F*inish the following sentence:

Being married to my spouse is like doing a summersault

because_____

What's the first thing that came to your mind? (Forget anything negative. The goal here is to be positive.)

…because I'm head over heels

…because I'm sometimes floored

…because no matter how we fall, we always find a way to roll with things

There's nothing magical about a summersault. Have fun with your spouse trying to finish your own phrases. Give a phrase to your spouse and ask your spouse to try to complete it. Follow up by asking your spouse to give you a phrase and you try to complete it.

Or play with some of these phrases:

Being married to you is like jumping in a pool

because _____

Being married to you is like blowing up a balloon

because _____

Being married to you is like opening a can of pickles

because _____

40 *Finish Your Spouse's Sentence*

41 ~ How Money Can Buy You Love

*A*lmost every day, you and your spouse spend money. What we usually strive for in our marriage is understanding, tolerance, and acceptance of each other's spending habits.

For example, if a wife knows that golf is important to her husband, she will try to accept that a certain portion of the family budget will be spent on clubs, fees, Golf Digest, and the annual trip to the big tournament.

When spouses don't reach an understanding, then money becomes a problem. When spouses accept each other's spending habits, then money is usually not a problem.

Do me favor, read the previous paragraph again. Do you see how in most marriages money is either a problem or not? In other words, it's either negative or neutral.

What about positive? Can't money be a source of love, an expression of intimacy in your marriage? I think it can. Here's how.

Go out and buy something that your spouse would normally buy. Spend money once this week the way your spouse normally spends it.

In other words, rather than just tolerating your spouse's spending habits and calling it quits at compatible, spend money this week in a way that will create a connection between you.

Imagine, in the example above, if that wife came home one day with a new box of the latest and greatest golf balls, just in time for the big tournament.

So you see, money can buy you love.

41 *Spend Money Like Your Spouse*

*E*very year I take each of my children away for a short two-day/one-night vacation. It's not a family trip or a father-children outing. Each trip is *one* of my kids and me.

I took one of my sons to a state park where we waded through the river. I took my other son bowling and to the zoo in Philadelphia. My oldest son and I took a trip to Cooperstown to the Baseball Hall of Fame. My daughter and I went to a working farm, where we milked the cows, collected eggs, and went for a hayride.

Each trip is two days of focused private time with *one* of my children. We eat together, play together, and enjoy a night in a hotel together.

Time with one child is completely different from family time, and it's obvious that it's special for them too.

So what's this have to do with your marriage?

I couldn't have done it without the cooperation and support of my wife. She had to agree, of course, to take care of the other kids while I disappear for two days. What an incredible gift she gave me—the gift of one-on-one time with each of my children!

Give your spouse the gift of one-on-one time with each of your children. Plan a special trip for them, book a night at a hotel, and take care of all the logistics at home so it's possible.

Being a good husband or wife includes empowering your spouse to be a great parent.

43 ～ SAY CHEESE PLEASE

W.D. Nesbit wrote:

> *The thing that goes the farthest towards making life worthwhile,*
> *That costs the least, and does the most, is just a pleasant smile.*
>
> *It's full of worth and goodness too, with manly kindness blent,*
> *It's worth a million dollars and it doesn't cost a cent."*

Your assignment is simple: make your spouse smile.

Think about it. What would your marriage be like if you and your spouse made each other smile at least once a day.

Life is full of stress, pressure, and responsibility. When we smile, it all melts away. Doesn't it? What a gift to give your spouse—a moment of refuge, a smile.

Of course, the challenge is how are you going to make your spouse smile?

You could tickle your spouse. That might be fun.

You could tell a joke. That will create a laughing smile. There's nothing wrong with a laughing smile. However, there's another kind of smile that's better. It's an *I'm touched* smile. You know the kind, right? It's the smile that comes over you when your soul is tickled.

Try putting a little post-it note on the inside of your spouse's cell phone. Write a sweet note and make a little picture. Then, shortly after your spouse leaves with phone in hand, phone your spouse. Your spouse will know who's calling even without caller ID.

Do you have any other ideas? Think about what would bring a smile to your spouse. A favorite chocolate packed in a lunch bag. A treat under the pillow. Hearing *your song* when your spouse walks through the door. An invitation to come into the bathroom where you have a candlelit bubble bath waiting.

You can do it. Make a plan and make your spouse smile this week.

43 *Bring a Smile to Your Spouse*

Conclusion

So there you have it, 43 quick and easy ways to make a good marriage great. None of them needs to be one-time events. I suggest you recycle them.

Even better than recycling them, pick some ideas and make them habits! Aristotle said, "Excellence is not an act; it's a habit."

My prayer for you is that you achieve excellence in your marriage—that it go from good to great.

43 Ways to Make a Good Marriage Great

1. Get Decked-out
2. Write a "Gratitude Letter"
3. Say "I Love You" in an Unforgettable Way
4. Give the Ultimate Hug
5. Extend a Kindness—Anonymously
6. Demonstrate Self Mastery
7. Sing a Song Together
8. Change Your Environment
9. Start a "Memories Box"
10. Slip Your Spouse a Note
11. Take a Walk Together
12. Say "Happy Anniversary"—Today!
13. Respond to Anger with Love

14. Read Aloud to Your Spouse

15. Compose a Poem Together

16. Extend an Act of Kindness

17. Tell Your Spouse a Joke

18. Play a Game Together

19. Solve a Problem Together

20. Give 5-Star Treatment

21. Do a Chore Together

22. Announce an Aspiration

23. Wear Your Spouse's Favorite

24. Ask for Your Favorite…

25. Button Your Spouse's Shirt

26. Find the Perfect Aphorism

27. Say "Thank You" Again

28. Show Affection Effectively

29. Clear the Air
30. Don't Hold Back
31. Make a Weekly Marriage Plan
32. Give Your Spouse Joy
33. Buy a Locket & Add a Photo
34. Clear Your Schedule
35. Complete a Puzzle Together
36. Improve Your Endings
37. Begin a Gratitude Journal
38. Express Appreciation Publicly
39. Let Your Spouse off the Hook
40. Finish Your Spouse's Sentence
41. Spend Money Like Your Spouse
42. Help Your Spouse be a Great Parent
43. Bring a Smile to Your Spouse

About the Author

MORT FERTEL burst onto the self-help stage in 1995 after working on Wall Street and studying with spiritual masters in Jerusalem and Thailand.

His breakthrough program, *Marriage Fitness*, has saved thousands of marriages and is endorsed by a full spectrum of clergy, self-help experts, and mental health professionals including Dr. Stephen Covey and Dr. John Gray.

Mort Fertel has appeared in the *New York Times, USA Today, Wall Street Journal, Family Circle, Ladies' Home Journal,* and *Psychology Today*. He was also a featured expert on nationally syndicated TV shows, Fox News Network, and a regular guest on talk radio.

Mort Fertel's client list includes celebrities, professional athletes, and CEOs. People from all walks of life seek his counsel on all matters of personal development including marriage, parenting, spirituality, weight loss, family budgeting, physical conditioning, and addictions.

Mort Fertel's unique brand of self-help integrates Eastern wisdom, Western philosophy, and biblical morality while offering step-by-step practical solutions to personal problems.

Mort Fertel graduated from the University of Pennsylvania, was the CEO of an international non-profit organization, and a former marathon runner. He lives with his wife and five children (including triplets!) in Baltimore, Maryland.

www.MortFertel.com

7 WEEKS TO THE MARRIAGE YOU REALLY WANT
The Marriage Fitness Tele-Boot Camp *with* Mort Fertel

All you need is a telephone and the desire to transform your marriage.

This is a home-based program. You don't have to go anywhere.

INCLUDES:

- 10 Tele-Seminars
- 1 Private phone session with Mort Fertel
- The Marriage Fitness Workbook and Personal Journal

- A complete 15 CD home learning system
- A members-only web site
- And much more

Choose from 2 tracks:

Duo Track available for couples.

Lone Ranger Track designed specifically for people dealing with an obstinate spouse.

Payment plans and discounts are available. *Satisfaction guaranteed.*

For more information, details, and the current schedule,

go to **www.MortFertel.com/tele-boot-camp.asp**

"Everyone laughed when I tried Change SOS;
but when I lost 35 pounds, quit smoking,
and retired my credit card debt..."

Change has never been so easy.

What do *you* want to change? How do *you* want to be different?

Whether you want a smaller waistline or a bigger bank account, more family time or less wasted time, now there's a *breakthrough* methodology for personal change. And it works every time.

Change SOS
Help for a New You

A Breakthrough Program for Personal Change
Completely Risk-Free & 100% Guaranteed to Work

www.ChangeSOS.com